Simple Machines
Everywhere

Simple Machines in Sports

Gillian Gosman

PowerKiDS
press™

New York

Published in 2015 by The Rosen Publishing Group, Inc.
29 East 21st Street, New York, NY 10010

First Edition

Book Design: Joe Carney
Photo Research: Katie Stryker

Photo Credits: Cover 0833379753/Shutterstock.com; p. 4 Lai leng Yiap/Hemera/Thinkstock; p. 5 tammykayphoto/Shutterstock.com; p. 6 Pavel Losevsky/Hemera/Thinkstock; p. 7 Markus Henttonen/Cultura/Getty Images; p. 8 Scott Leman/iStock/Thinkstock; p. 9 Doug Peterson/iStock/Thinkstock; p. 10 sirichai_raksue/iStock/Thinkstock; p. 11 (top) Craig Hill/Shutterstock.com; p. 11 (bottom) Reid Harrington/iStock/Thinkstock; p. 12 diego_cervo/iStock/Thinkstock; p. 14 irman/iStock/Thinkstock; p. 15 Minerva Studio/Shutterstock.com; p. 16 Jupiterimages/Stockbyte/Thinkstock; p. 17 Adie Bush/Cultura/Getty Images; p. 18 Natursports/Shutterstock.com; p. 20 LexussK/iStock/Thinkstock; p. 21 Jacopo Raule/Getty Images; p. 22 Monkey Business Images/Shutterstock.com.

Library of Congress Cataloging-in-Publication Data

Gosman, Gillian.
Simple machines in sports / by Gillian Gosman. — First edition.
    pages cm. — (Simple machines everywhere)
Includes index.
ISBN 978-1-4777-6829-7 (library binding) — ISBN 978-1-4777-6830-3 (pbk.) — ISBN 978-1-4777-6640-8 (6-pack)
1. Sports—Equipment and supplies—Juvenile literature. 2. Machines—Juvenile literature. I. Title.
GV745.G67 2015
688.7'6—dc23
                              2013046682

Manufactured in the United States of America

CPSIA Compliance Information: Batch #WS14PK5: For Further Information contact Rosen Publishing, New York, New York at 1-800-237-9932

Contents

What Is a Simple Machine?

Simple machines are everywhere! A baseball bat, a skateboard, and a soccer cleat each work because of the power of a different simple machine. Simple machines are tools that help us do all kinds of work by multiplying, or increasing, the amount of **effort**, or force, we apply to a job. The greater the force applied, the more **motion** will result.

The six different simple machines are the inclined plane, wedge, screw, lever, pulley, and wheel and **axle**. Your favorite athletes use simple machines, and their bodies can also serve as examples of simple machines. Simple machines help athletes turn **potential energy** into **kinetic energy**.

Wedges are very useful tools. You might have used a doorstop to keep a door open. A doorstop is a wedge.

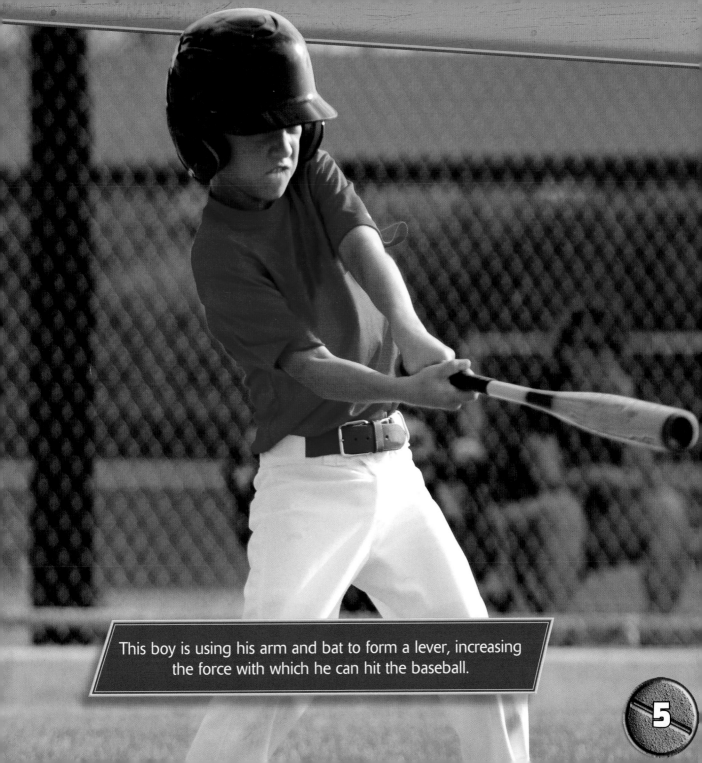

This boy is using his arm and bat to form a lever, increasing the force with which he can hit the baseball.

It's Plane to See

An inclined plane is a flat, tilted **surface** with one end that is higher than the other. An inclined plane's **slope** is how tilted it is. Pushing or pulling an object up or down an inclined plane requires less **effort** than lifting or lowering the object.

The steeper an inclined plane's slope is, the more effort it takes to move things, or yourself, up it.

Rise

Run

The distance an inclined plane rises is called its rise, while its horizontal length is its run. To get the plane's slope, divide its rise by its run.

Inclined planes are found in many sports. The slope of a hill forms a great inclined plane for downhill skiing. A skateboard ramp works the same way! In both sports, the inclined plane allows the athlete to travel with less effort and at faster speeds than could be done on a flat surface.

A Wedge Gives You an Edge

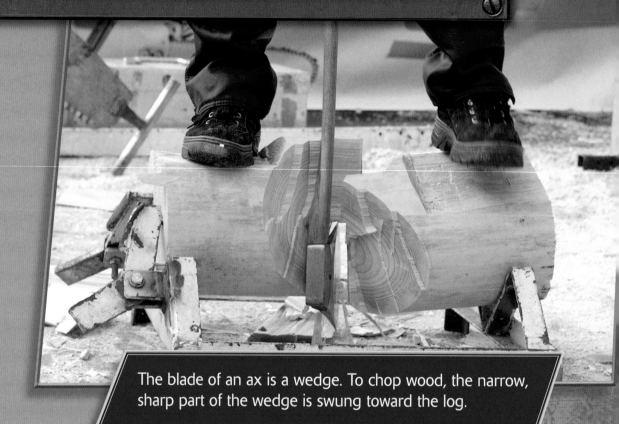

The blade of an ax is a wedge. To chop wood, the narrow, sharp part of the wedge is swung toward the log.

Wedges are used to cut objects or to hold them in place. You insert a wedge's **narrow** edge into an object. The effort you put into driving the wedge into the object is multiplied and redirected sideways.

Ice skates allow you to glide over ice because the blade is a wedge. The narrow edge cuts through the ice, moving you forward with ease. Now imagine yourself running in a pair of soccer cleats. Cleats are wedges used to hold the shoe in place in the ground so the runner doesn't slip.

These shoes have wedge-shaped cleats on the bottoms. The wedges are driven into the ground when the players run. This keeps them from slipping on the grass.

That's Some Screw!

A screw is a thin **cylindrical** bar. A wood screw is flat at one end and pointed at the other end. There is a ridge, called a thread, which runs around the shaft. The thread is a spiraled inclined plane. To use a screw, force is applied to the flat end, and the screw is twisted into an object. The thread multiplies the effort, lifting the material around it. When the screw is in place, the thread is wedged into the material, holding it in place.

Screws hold basketball backboards together. You can also find them on the mouths of water bottles.

Here, you can see the threads around these screws. Using a screwdriver, screws are twisted into place. Screw guns are also used to make screwing even easier!

Thread

The thread around this water bottle's mouth allows the top to be screwed on. This keeps the water from leaking out so there is plenty for you to drink!

Screws are used to hold together sports equipment and accessories. Here, you can see the screws holding on the wheels of this skateboard.

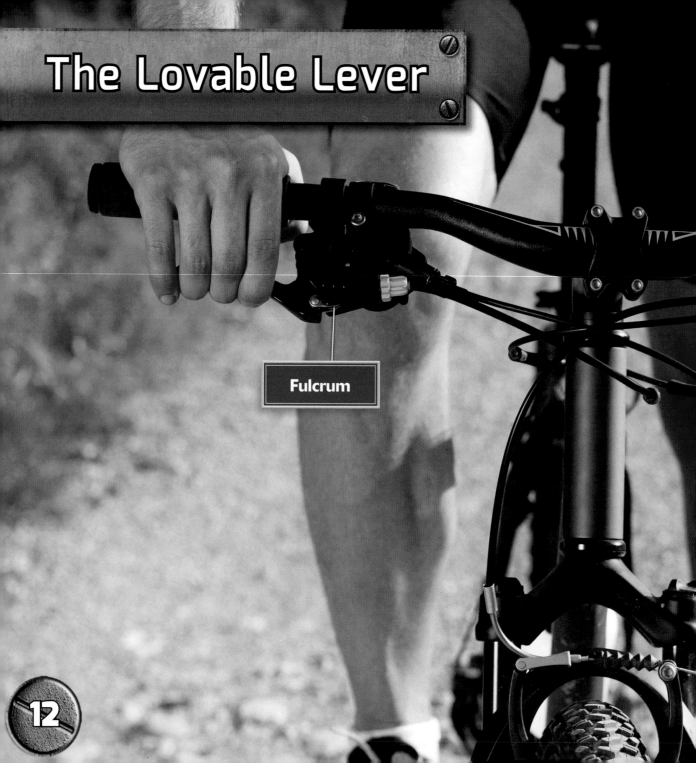

The Lovable Lever

Fulcrum

In this picture, you can see the bicyclist gripping the brakes. This pulls the brake cables taut and presses the brake pads against the wheels of the bike.

Fulcrum

A lever is a straight plank that **pivots** on a fixed point called the fulcrum. Levers are used to lift, push, or pull. The lever multiplies the effort put into it.

Levers are grouped into three classes. A lever's class depends on where the fulcrum is in relation to the load and effort and on the direction in which effort is applied. In a first-class lever, the fulcrum sits between the effort and the load, and effort is applied down. Bicycle hand brakes are first-class levers. Effort is applied by pressing down the bar that pivots on a fulcrum. This tightens the brake cable and stops the wheel.

Levers Have Class!

This man is using his arms to apply effort and lift the load of his body. His feet are the fulcrum. Over time, push-ups will strengthen his arms and core muscles.

The fulcrum of a second-class lever is at one end of a plank. Effort is applied upward at the other end. When doing push-ups, your body works like a second-class lever. The fulcrum is at your feet, the load is your body weight, and your arms apply the effort.

The fulcrum and the load in a third-class lever sit at opposite ends of the plank. Effort is applied in the middle. When swinging a baseball bat, your arm and bat form a lever. The load is the ball, and it is driven forward with the force provided by the effort of your arm muscles.

This woman is using her body as a lever to push herself away from the foot platform. Many types of fitness machines use levers.

Fulcrum

Effort

Load

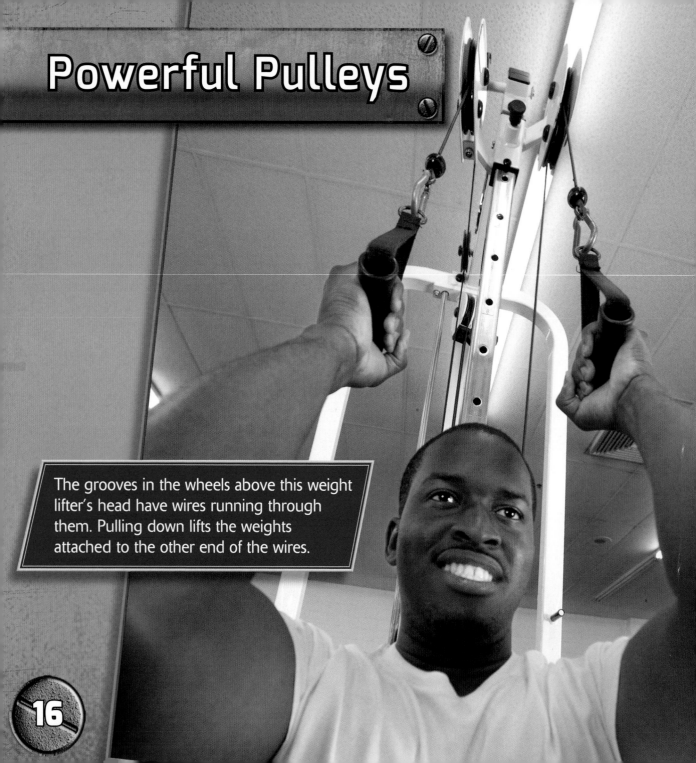

Powerful Pulleys

The grooves in the wheels above this weight lifter's head have wires running through them. Pulling down lifts the weights attached to the other end of the wires.

A pulley is a wheel that turns on an axle. There is often a groove along the outer edge of the wheel. A rope, chain, or cable runs along this groove. One end of the rope, chain, or cable is attached to a load. Effort is applied to the other end to raise the load. Pulleys can be fixed in place, or they can move along the length of the rope.

You can find pulleys in many machines used for weight lifting. Fixed pulleys allow athletes to raise and lower very heavy weights safely and, in doing so, build muscles.

Pulleys are very important tools for rock climbers. They use pulleys to pull themselves up and to rappel down.

The Wheel Deal

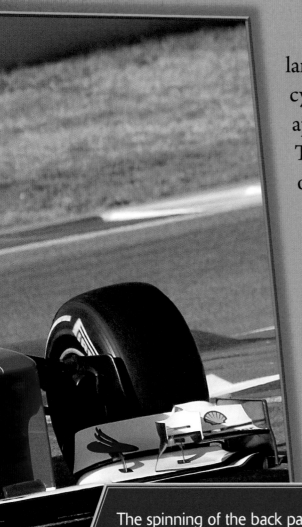

A wheel and axle is made up of a large wheel that is attached to a smaller cylindrical rod called an axle. Effort is applied to make the axle rotate, or turn. This effort is multiplied in the turning of the larger wheel.

A bicycle wheel is a large circle of metal. Spokes meet at the axle at its center, which is held in place by long arms of metal extending down from the main frame. Effort is applied by turning the foot pedals, which in turn rotate the **gears**. A chain connects the gears to the rear wheel.

The spinning of the back pair of this Formula One race car's wheels is what makes the car speed around the track.

Not So Simple After All!

This boy's bike contains several simple machines. The hill that he is on is a simple machine, too. It is an inclined plane.

A compound or **complex** machine is one made up of two or more simple machines. Complex machines are common in life and in sports. Humans have invented countless, increasingly complex machines!

Consider the bicycle. As we've learned, its hand brake is a lever, and it rolls on its wheels and axles. Moreover, the bicycle's frame is held together in part by screws.

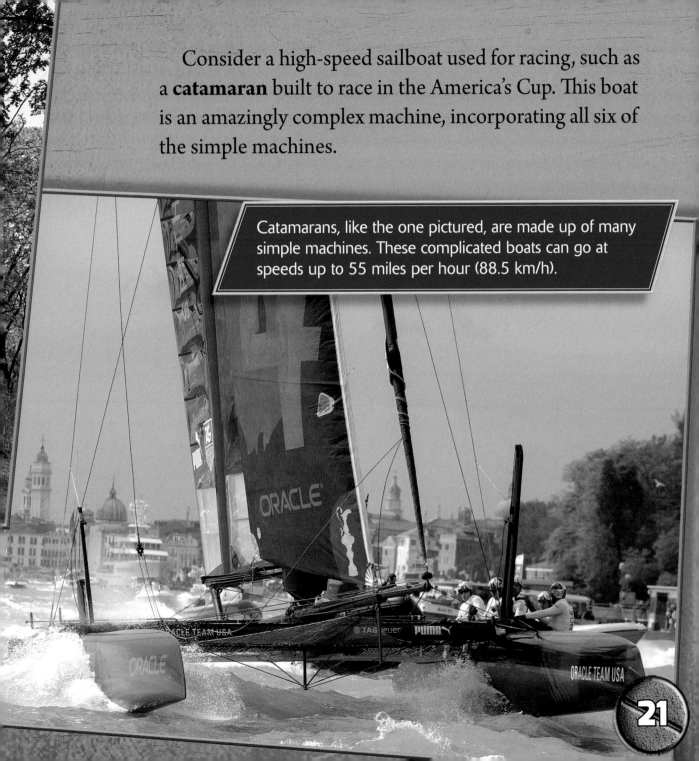

Consider a high-speed sailboat used for racing, such as a **catamaran** built to race in the America's Cup. This boat is an amazingly complex machine, incorporating all six of the simple machines.

Catamarans, like the one pictured, are made up of many simple machines. These complicated boats can go at speeds up to 55 miles per hour (88.5 km/h).

Simple Success

Without simple machines, our lives would be extremely simple. We would have no tools with which to prepare food, to travel with speed, or to build shelters.

Simple machines are also important to the sports we love to play and watch. The human body can do great things. With the help of simple machines, though, we have discovered many ways to test and develop our natural abilities on the field, on the court, on land, and at sea. What will we think of next? Perhaps it is up to you. Choose a simple machine, and invent the next great sport!

Simple machines make sports fun! Cleats keep soccer players on their feet, running and kicking.

Glossary

axle (AK-sul) A bar or a shaft on which a wheel or a pair of wheels turns.

catamaran (ka-tuh-muh-RAN) A sailboat with two hulls and a structure that connects them.

complex (kom-PLEKS) Made up of many connected parts.

cylindrical (suh-LIN-drih-kul) Shaped like a cylinder.

effort (EH-fert) The amount of force applied to an object.

gears (GEERZ) Parts of a machine that help it work.

kinetic energy (kuh-NEH-tik EH-ner-jee) The energy of motion.

motion (MOH-shun) Movement.

narrow (NER-oh) Not very wide.

pivots (PIH-vuts) Turns on a fixed point.

potential energy (puh-TEN-shul EH-nur-jee) Work that a thing might do.

slope (SLOHP) A hill.

surface (SER-fes) The outside of anything.

Index

A

axle(s), 4, 17, 19–20

B

bar, 10, 13

E

effort, 4, 6–8, 10, 13,
    14–15, 17, 19

F

force, 4, 10, 15

fulcrum, 13–15

I

inclined plane(s), 4,
    6–7, 10

K

kinetic energy, 4

L

lever(s), 4, 13–15, 20

load, 13–15, 17

P

plank, 13, 14–15

potential energy, 4

pulley(s), 4, 17

S

screw(s), 4, 10, 20

slope, 6–7

surface, 6–7

T

tool(s), 4, 22

W

wedge(s), 4, 8–9

Websites

Due to the changing nature of Internet links, PowerKids Press has developed an online list of websites related to the subject of this book. This site is updated regularly. Please use this link to access the list:

www.powerkidslinks.com/sme/sport/